The Road to a Happy Life

By

Dr. Pradeep K. Chadha

MBBS. DCP. DPM.

Raider Publishing International

New York   London   Swansea

ISBN: 1-934360-21-X
Published By Raider Publishing International
www.RaiderPublishing.com
New York London Swansea

Printed in the United States of America and the United Kingdom
By Lightning Source Ltd.

Other Books By Dr. Chadha
The Stress Barrier: Nature's Way to Overcoming Stress

ABOUT THE AUTHOR

Pradeep Chadha trained as a medical doctor in India. He then moved to Ireland where he trained as a psychiatrist and hypnotherapist, before setting-up his practice in Dublin. He now specialises in the drugless treatment of psychiatric conditions. In his work with patients and clients, Pradeep integrates the modern science of the West with the spiritual science and wisdom of the East. He also applies the wider laws of Nature to solve problems in individual lives.

He has also written:

The Stress Barrier
(Nature's Way to Overcoming Stress)
Published by Blackhall Publishing, Dublin, 1999
ISBN 1-901657-65-5

He can be contacted through his website:
www.drpkchadha.com

To...

He who is known by different names in different ages
My guide, my master, my teacher and my father.

Also to

Mr. Harbans Lal Bhambri

And in remembrance of

Mrs. Shobha Bhambri

Mrs. Prem Lata Chadha

ACKNOWLEGEMENTS

I thank my parents, my wife Rita and our children Virat, Kunwar, Shaleen and Chirag, for making this book possible.

Thanks are also due to Gráinne Murphy for preparing the initial draft and to Dermot Peavoy who helped me in editing the final text.

Contents

The Road to a Happy Life

By

Dr. Pradeep K. Chadha
MBBS. DCP. DPM.

INTRODUCTION

This book is a distillation of my learning experiences in personal growth, stress management and mental health. It summarises the knowledge I have gleaned from many years working with people as a psychiatrist and hypnotherapist.

Most of the time people have answers to their own problems, but they do not know this. It is my hope that this book will help readers to solve problems in their own day-to-day lives.

Though divided into nine sections, each page stands alone, independent of the rest of the book, to give the reader an insight into at least one aspect of life.

It is not therefore necessary to read the book sequentially, from cover to cover. The reader may dip into it on any page, at any time, as often as desired.

I would like readers to be aware that wherever I use the word 'scripture' in the book, I am drawing upon an unspecified great spiritual text from any one of many faiths and cultures.

-     Pradeep K Chadha

How
To
Enrich
Your
Family Life

BEING CHILDLIKE

We can learn a lot from a child.
As we grow up, we sometimes forget to scream, to
laugh, to cry and to live with what nature has
given us. To a child these things come easily and
effortlessly.

Children have a tendency to live life easily. They can laugh, cry or scream spontaneously without thinking of social "norms" or consequences.

As we grow up, societal expectations encourage us to forget our childlike qualities. We then lose our spontaneity. If we regain these qualities, while balancing them against the prevalent culture of the time, life becomes easier and more effortless.

ENCOURAGE CHILDREN TO EXPERIMENT

Children learn from their own experiences, rather than the verbal advice of grown-ups. If we could help them to experiment, we would have fewer regrets as parents.

Instead of *telling* children what to do in a particular situation, it is far better to *offer an opinion* about a possible alternative.

No matter what parents say, children will make their own mistakes; and they will learn from their mistakes themselves, in their own time.

If they can be encouraged to experiment, children will tend to have more respect for their parents.

FAMILY

A family is the microcosm of the universal family,
where God is the supreme head.

We find similar natural laws operating at every level, throughout the universe. The social structure of a troop of monkeys, or of a colony of ants or termites, resembles that of a human community.

Similarly, the universal family, with God as its head, resembles the structure of a human family. For various issues, each human family has a main decision-maker, on whose decisions the growth of the family depends.

INVESTING IN CHILDREN

We spend most of our lives accumulating savings or pensions to see us through our later years. How much of that time could have been invested in bringing more happiness into our children's lives, while they were still young?

Life expectancy after retirement is often but a few years. In order to build up savings and pensions for this short period, we work hard in our younger days. A lot more of that time could possibly be invested in bringing extra happiness into the lives of our children.

Time invested in our children is far more worthwhile than doing extra work to gain more money.

Such an investment brings dividends for many generations. Our children, as a result of it are secure, more confident and more positive in life.

LEGACY TO CHILDREN

Without being aware of it, we pass on a lot more to our children than our wealth. We also pass on our anxieties, fears, insecurities and anger.

We normally think of inheritance in terms of money and property, passed on from one generation to the next. It is not generally appreciated that our children also inherit our emotional make-up.

Our feelings are an involuntary part of their legacy.

Children who come from a secure, nourishing environment are confident.

Children who experience fear, depression and anger in their parents, pick up these emotions and hold on to them.

LOSS

Loss is the experience of letting go of anyone – or anything – that we take for granted. It is usually forced upon us by circumstances.

If life is a journey, then loss is the process of parting company with fellow travellers. The longer we travel with them and the closer they are to us, the deeper is the sense of loss. Even so, this sense of loss is only temporary and it passes.

We must then continue our life's journey with new travelling companions; and as our journey continues, it is inevitable that we will meet other travellers – people who may be strangers to us now.

Let us enjoy our fellow travellers. They are gifts of Nature.

If we become aware of the privileges bestowed by our present companions – and by those we have yet to meet – our pain at any eventual loss will be lessened.

PARENTING

If we give our children safety, security and lots of time, they will grow up to be secure, generous and forgiving.

Parenting is a skill most parents lack.

Children are brought up with parental skills passed down from their grandparents.

Mistakes are too often repeated, although they are sometimes rectified by a younger generation's child-rearing methods.

Secure and generous children are a credit to everyone – their parents, their society and their country.

RESPECTING CHILDREN

We need to treat our children with as much respect as we would like to receive ourselves, from God.

Our world is governed by adults. Laws for the welfare of children are made by adults.

We are all also the children of God. Laws have been made for us by the Lord.

Some of us don't think of asking ourselves, when we treat our children disrespectfully, how it would be if the Lord – our lawmaker and parent – did the same to us. Then how would we feel?

RESPECTING OURSELVES

*It is remarkable that the more we respect
ourselves, the more we accept and respect others.*

Others are mirrors of ourselves.

We unconsciously see in others what we have within ourselves.

If we are fearful, we become afraid of others without reason.

If we accept ourselves, we are more accepting of others. So we are less critical of them.

SKILFUL PARENTING

A skilful parent is like an umbrella.
An umbrella protects us from too much sun or rain
without troubling us.
Likewise, parents can keep a watchful eye on their
children, protecting them from hurt or damage,
while letting them learn and grow up with minimal
interference.

We can become truly good parents only if we are living examples of goodness.

Self-confidence, self-respect, high self-esteem and wisdom, for instance, are qualities of goodness. They make us better individuals.

Having more of these qualities helps us to pass them on to our children.

Controlling and authoritative parents may have had fearful upbringings themselves. Naturally, they pass on these characteristics to their children.

SPENDING TIME
WITH CHILDREN

For many parents, caring for a child means
providing for their material needs.
They may consider time spent with the child to be
of secondary importance.
For a child, however, the safety and love they feel,
just by being with the parent, matters more than
toys.

'Quality time' is a phrase often used by parents – probably with a sense of guilt – to describe the time they spend with their children.

Children identify themselves with their parents. They consider themselves to be part of their mother, for instance, if she is the full-time carer.

The time that parents spend with their children is therefore important for their emotional growth.

Toys provide stimulation for intellectual growth only.

*Making
The
Best
Of
Your
Personal Life*

ACCEPTANCE

Acceptance is the key that opens the door to change.

We tend to make the mistake of fighting against what we need to change. We see it as our enemy. We resist it.

A better approach would be to respect and accept it. It is only when we do so that we can take the steps required to resolve our present situation.

Without acceptance, we make life difficult for ourselves.

AMBITION

When used constructively, anger and fear make us ambitious. Ambition makes us strive to fulfil our needs. It is no coincidence that when anger and fear are gone, our needs become fewer.

It is an amazing fact that the drive of ambition is a measure of anger and fear.

The more fearful and angry we are the more power we tend to seek.

Money is the usual goal of the ambitious – as it gives them power that can lead to worldly or material success.

When our ambition is fulfilled, our sense of contentment usually increases.

CARING FOR OURSELVES

*It is our responsibility to look after ourselves.
Doing so helps us to fulfil our duties to our
families and to society at large.
However, to look after one's own interests, at the
expense of others, is selfish.*

Many people think it is selfish to look after themselves. However, it is as much their duty to look after themselves, as it is to care for others.

'Selfish' is an appropriate description only for those who neglect or harm others, in looking after themselves.

Unless and until we are happy and healthy ourselves, it is impossible for us to create happiness for others.

It is important to realise there are limits to how much we can be stretched, in doing duty for others.

COMPETING WITH OURSELVES

It is far better to compete with ourselves than to compete with others.
Challenging ourselves makes us aware of our own limitations.

Probably the best competitor we have is ourselves.

Competing with others and losing, creates a humiliating sense of defeat.

Winning the competition makes others lose and this creates jealousy.

Competing with ourselves makes us winners in two ways:

1. If we reach our goals we are winners through our own achievements; and we can compliment ourselves.

2. If we are unable to achieve our goals, we simply learn from our mistakes; and we are not humiliated in the eyes of others.

CRYING BALANCES US

Crying is an excellent emotional exercise. It helps us to finish our emotional work. It also helps to balance our nervous and hormonal systems.

When we are stressed-out, our bodies are in fighting mode.

In this state, our bodies feel that crying or any form of emotional expression would be a luxury.

However, when we relax, that part of our nervous system associated with crying becomes activated.

Crying is a sign of emotional expression. Afterwards, our nervous and endocrine systems become balanced.

DECISION-MAKING

When we are stressed-out, we can often see only one choice. The more relaxed we are, the more choices we have.

A stressed-out individual becomes focused on an issue to the extent of becoming blinkered. This creates a sense of desperation, along with an inability to see a wider perspective.

When this happens, the first choice that comes to mind is taken up as the only choice.

As the individual becomes relaxed and patient, a wider picture starts to appear.

This wider picture brings up more choices. These are choices the person is unable to imagine in the stressed state.

The more relaxed a person becomes, the more choices they have.

DEFENSIVENESS

*All our defence mechanisms, like telling lies and
avoiding certain situations, are reflections of our
confidence. We need psychological defences when
we lack inner confidence.
A secure person feels confident with no
compulsion to be defensive.*

Anger and fear are the core reasons for lack of
confidence in ourselves. Our self-esteem is low in
proportion to the strength of these emotions in us.

Low self-esteem also results in aggression and
hostility.

When we get rid of anger and fear (instead of
suppressing these feelings), our confidence rises
spontaneously.

We then start behaving in a positive way.

EMOTIONS AND BEHAVIOUR

Our behaviour is determined by our emotions.
Think of the last time you felt angry with someone.
How did you behave with that person?
Now remember the last time you felt love for
someone. How did you behave then?

Experience shows that our emotions lie behind our behaviour. In other words, our behaviour is determined by our emotional make-up.

If we feel hatred for someone, our behaviour will reflect that feeling, despite all efforts to mask it.

If we feel love towards someone, our behaviour will reveal that too – without our being aware of it.

Our emotions control our behaviour.

EXERCISE FOR SUCCESS

Doing the following exercise will help you to achieve success in almost anything.

1. Close your eyes and relax.

2. Imagine that you have achieved your goal.

3. Introduce the colours, sounds, smells, touch and taste, that you might experience on achieving your goal.

4. Take your time in letting this experience sink into your mind.

5. Open your eyes.

Repeat this exercise at random, over days, weeks and months – until your goal is achieved.

FEAR

Fear drives an animal to survive. But remaining fearful when there is no longer any threat only makes us stressed out and insecure.

A fearful animal attacks when cornered. The energy that fear produces in our bodies propels us out of a trouble spot. Thus fear is a gift from nature to help animals to flee and avoid danger.

However, repetitive fearful experiences train our nervous systems to continue perceiving fear, even in neutral situations.

Paradoxically, while this drive may help us to gain more social, political and physical power, it also makes us feel more insecure.

Holding onto underlying fears makes us anxious. But when we face up to our fears and allow them to die their own natural deaths, we feel more secure.

Thereby we end up stronger.

FORMS OF ANGER

*Anger manifests itself in many forms – annoyance,
jealousy, guilt, irritability and frustration.*

Anger is a feeling of unease in response to a situation that we would like to reverse. It can occur in a mild form, like annoyance, jealousy or irritability.

Guilt is experienced when we direct anger and fear at ourselves.

Frustration is experienced when anger has been unexpressed for some time.

GIVING AND FORGIVING

People who believe in "giving," are also "forgiving."

Forgiveness is a sign of generosity.

People may pose as generous, but may only be 'people pleasers'.

Such people tend to be less forgiving than those who are genuinely generous.

People who are charitable are genuinely forgiving.

A 'miser' would usually be unforgiving.

GOODNESS DEEP WITHIN

Amazingly, goodness lies buried in us all beneath our negative emotions of anger, hurt, guilt and jealousy.
It requires courage to plumb our own depths, to release that goodness.

Many of us have done exercises with affirmations and positive thinking. They are helpful, but only to a point.

When we have negative emotions inside us, positive affirmations cannot push them away.

It is only when we let go of our negative emotions that we are able to feel positive. The goodness within us is then revealed. Affirmations and positive thinking practices then become wonderfully unnecessary.

LEARNED HELPLESSNESS

*Isn't it interesting that helplessness is learned?
People suffer from depression as a result. Some
find it hard to believe that helplessness can be
unlearned as spontaneously as it is learned.*

Seligman's name is well known in research on helplessness. He discovered that our depression results from learned helplessness.

Helplessness can be unlearned as easily as we learn it. But unlearning it requires skills that need constant practice.

LIVING OUR OWN LIVES

Most people spend most of their lives trying to live up to other people's expectations.
Yet we would all prefer to live according to our own desires. The few who do, become leaders in their own fields.

Most of the misery in people's lives is due to a lack of freedom to do what they want to do.

They want to be happy. But societal and parental expectations make them slaves to the wishes of others.

If they fail to live up to the expectations of others – as often happens – they become miserable. Since they also fail to live up to their own desires – they become twice as miserable.

Those of us who develop the skills to live life without these hang-ups choose our own paths.

Such people are called 'leaders'.

MEDITATION

Anything done slowly, with full focus and minimum stimulation, is a form of meditation.

The characteristic quality of meditation is the minimising of sensory stimulation.

Even farmers and gardeners meditate, simply by working on the land with a focused mind.

Because the work involved is slow, with little sensory stimulation, such activities are relaxing.

Activities that minimise stimulation similarly, are meditative in nature.

NECESSARY DEPENDENCE

*Dependence on our elders, teachers and guides is
necessary to enable us to become physically,
intellectually and emotionally independent.*

It is virtually impossible to become independent
without being dependent on others, at least for a while. This
dependence strengthens us.

We depend on our parents to make us physically
stronger; and on our teachers to make us intellectually self-
reliant.

Similarly, we need guides to help us become
emotionally independent.

Independence without initial dependence on our
elders and guides is impossible to achieve.

PURPOSE OF LIFE

What is the purpose of life?
I don't know.
Do you?

People have spent lifetimes seeking the answer to this question. Yet the answer remains elusive.

Some people believe they are born to suffer. Some believe they are born to rule others. Some believe they are born to serve others.

Yet everyone wants to feel happy and to enjoy life; and we all do so in our own personal ways.

If only we could enjoy life comfortably, with fewer physical needs; and if we could spread this sense of happiness to others, in our own individual ways; then the purpose of life would surely be served.

SELF-ACCEPTANCE EXERCISE

The following exercise will help you to accept yourself.

1. Stand in front of a mirror.

2. Look at your reflection.

3. Say to your reflection whatever you want to say about yourself – pleasant and unpleasant.

4. In your mind at the end, say to your reflection: 'I accept you the way you are'.

You may surprise yourself by what you feel.

This is a simple exercise. It will make you aware of how accepting or unaccepting you are of yourself.

If you can accept yourself, you will be in total command of your own life and destiny.

TIME OF OUR LIVES

Nature sees Time as irrelevant.
For us it is important because we feel we have
short lifespans.

Time is the fourth dimension along with length, width and height.

Accordingly, as lives are naturally created and destroyed, dimensions lose their meaning in the course of the natural creation and destruction of life.

Dimensions exist only as long as the entity to which they belong exists; and then they are no more.

We lack a sense of the time that existed before we were born, or that will continue after we die.

We give importance only to the 'time of our lives' – the time that passes during our own lifespans.

As the dimensions of length, width and height are destroyed with each entity, so is time.

LOVE YOURSELF

When you start loving yourself you can also begin to love others, without wanting love in return.

Love is generally 'exchanged' between people.

Sometimes, people who have not received enough love feel the need to be given more.

When we have experienced 'abundant' love we can give it to others generously.

Only then can love be 'given' without expecting it in return.

This is unconditional love.

Some
Open
Secrets
About
Work Life

AUTHORITY FIGURES

*A fearful authority figure creates fear, an angry
one creates anger.*
A cheerful superior creates a sense of comfort.
*A happy person in power creates a sense of growth
and happiness.*

People who become leaders in any sphere of life
attain an image of authority. They create the same emotions
in the people they lead, as they themselves have.

A comfortable, happy leader generates happiness in
others.

MANAGEMENT

Successful management of a family, a corporation or a country, follows the same principles that the Lord has set down for the Universe:
- Make ground rules.
- Familiarise people with their responsibilities.
- Give them freedom to act.
- Sit back and supervise.

Invisibility and minimal interference make management efficient.

As in everything else, the best management follows Nature's ways.

One of the scriptures says that the best management is least management.

The purpose of management is to oversee things, so that they run smoothly. If things run smoothly, there is hardly anything to manage.

Visibility and interference are necessary only when something has to be changed.

MEANING OF SUCCESS

'Success' has different meanings for everyone.
Those who achieve wealth, academic success and
fame are said to be successful.
But how many of us are successful in attaining
happiness and contentment?

In the present-day world, success is popularly measured by many different parameters.

High earnings, fame and glamour, are widely thought to be the attributes of success.

Yet many 'successful' people with these attributes are unhappy.

Very few of us are successful in attaining happiness and contentment.

True success requires a balance between material comforts and mental happiness.

TIME MANAGEMENT

1. Write down tasks that have to be performed.

2. Prioritise them.

3. Write them down again in priority order.

4. Decide on an appropriate time for their completion.

5. Taking rest periods into account, write down the finishing time/date after each task.

6. Implement these tasks, without burning yourself out.

How
To
Deal
With
Mental Health
Issues

DEPRESSION

Behind every depressed person is a tale of anger,
loss or trauma.

Clinical experience shows that depression results from unfinished emotional expression. Our anger, when unexpressed and suppressed, results in depression.

An unfinished grief process and the effects of traumatic experiences are other causes of depression.

Holding on to negative and painful emotions, disturbs the neurochemical balance in our bodies. This creates depression.

DEALING WITH FEARS AND PHOBIAS

In order to deal with any fear, take the following steps.

1. Sit comfortably on a chair.

2. Close your eyes.

3. Recall the fearful event *fast*, from start to finish.

4. Repeat it many times.

5. Do it every day if needed.

Continue doing it until you become comfortable with the situation.

DEALING WITH ISSUES FROM YOUR PAST

To deal with any issue that bothers you from your past, do the following exercise.

1. Close your eyes and recall the incident from start to finish, as fast as you can go through it.

2. Do it again.

3. Do it again and again and again, until you become comfortable with it.

Some restlessness, anger and sadness may be experienced in the process.

DEALING WITH OBSESSIONS

An easy way to get rid of obsessions is to do the following exercise repetitively.

1. Close your eyes.

2. Contemplate all the thoughts that force themselves into your mind.

3. Without fighting them or dwelling on them, let them come and let them go.

4. Continue doing this until your mind becomes blank or thoughtless.

5. Then open your eyes.

Do the above exercise as often and for as long as needed.

GRIEVING EXERCISE

This simple exercise will be effective in bringing us through grief.

1. Close your eyes.

2. Imagine seeing the person you have lost.

3. In your mind, say to the person what you always wanted to say.

4. Bid "goodbye" and imagine seeing the person go.

5. Let your feelings be experienced.

Repeat the exercise many times over a few days, until you are happy to let the person go.

GUILT

If a sense of guilt is intense, it is often perceived as a 'sin'. Guilt can also torture us to the grave. It is possible, however, to free ourselves of this scourge.

We can fall into the trap of guilt or self-blame, even if we have made no mistake.

The trap is laid by insecurity, low self-esteem and fear. It is reinforced by anger with oneself and fear of the imagined consequences of our actions.

When we successfully work through our self-anger, the guilt dissipates. We are then free of the trap.

If we are confident in ourselves, mistakes are seen as such – without any sense of guilt.

HABITS AND ADDICTIONS

*All bad habits, including addictions, arise from
unresolved emotional issues.
Burn out the emotions involved and you can be
free of the habit.*

Habits and addictions are behavioural effects of unfulfilled emotional needs.

Insecurity, a craving for attention and low self esteem, are some of the negative emotions that draw people into addiction.

They feel that their addictions fulfil inner needs not met by their relationships, or by other aspects of their lives.

Letting go of the negative emotions brings a sense of security and minimises those unmet inner needs.

MENTAL FREEDOM

Good mental health is all about mental freedom.
The healthier we are, the more we feel free.
Mental ill-health comes from making ourselves
slaves to thoughts and feelings that we hold on to
for too long.

Mental ill-health creates a sense of losing control. A person loses control over his or her own life.

The loss of control extends to the person's own environment and they become dependent on others.

Dependence on medication is one indication of a loss of freedom.

A person can become independent by freeing themselves from anger and fear.

One of the major causes of mental ill-health is the inability to let go of our feelings and emotions.

MENTAL SLAVERY

Emotional slavery is mental slavery.
Freedom from it is the core requirement for inner freedom.
People with freedom in their hearts and minds have helped others attain freedom from political slavery.

Slavery and freedom also exist in the mind.

Enslaved thinking is the product of emotional slavery.

Holding on to our fears makes us behave and think like slaves.

People may be free politically, but they behave like slaves if they feel and think like slaves.

An inner sense of freedom comes only with emotional freedom.

How
To
Deal
With
Stress

EARNING RELAXATION

The state of relaxation has to be earned.
The only investment one needs is time, given
exclusively to ourselves, every day of our lives.

Relaxation is an active process. We sometimes believe it will come to us simply by engaging in a different activity.

However, we have to 'work' towards relaxation, to feel relaxed. We have to 'earn' our relaxation.

In order to spend money, we have to earn it.

Likewise, we can earn that state of mind we call relaxation. The more we 'earn' it and the less we 'spend' it, the more it accumulates.

ONE-MINUTE RELAXATION

- When you are stressed-out, join the palms of your hands together.
- Breathe out to empty your lungs.
- Hold your breath.
- Then push your two palms against each other for as long as you can.
- When you become breathless, loosen your palms and take in a deep breath.
- Regain your normal breathing pattern.
- Repeat as many times as needed.

OVER-STIMULATION

If we continue to live a life of stimulation, if we are 'on the go' all the time, we then find it hard to sit down without engaging in any mental or physical activity.

Unknown to us, our body then undergoes active wear and tear, with no time to repair itself.

Therefore, we need skills to stop mental and physical activities, intermittently, throughout the day.

These skills help our body to recover quickly from the wear and tear it undergoes.

CONTROL

*People who must control their lives strive hard.
People who have control over their lives are easy-
going.*

Clinical experience shows that most people who come into therapy, with various mental conditions, have a tendency to try to control their lives.

Their struggle with control makes them "fight" harder. The harder they fight, the more difficult it becomes to gain control. Eventually, they "cannot cope" and seek help.

As treatment proceeds, they become easy-going and regain control over their lives.

PROLONGED STRESS

Prolonged stress leads to the destruction of any family, corporation, society, country or individual.

The mind perceives stress as a threat to existence.

This sense of threat has to be dealt with as a priority, before growth can begin.

Prolonged stress has only one outcome – death.

Stress can be dealt with by measures that will relax our body systems, to diminish their state of stress.

Desperate measures only create more stress.

A relaxed individual will best lead a family, a corporation, a society or a country, out of any stressful situation.

RELAXATION

*Physical relaxation, when combined with
emotional relaxation, brings a sense of confidence
and raises self-esteem.
We then trust more in Nature and in ourselves. We
also become more accepting of others. This brings
about contentment.*

Relaxation is a state of mind.
It results from constant and regular practice.
We can attain it only by disciplining ourselves.

If we postpone relaxation for long, we will
experience stress in our lives.

RELAXATION EXERCISE

To relax quickly, take in a deep breath.
Pause.
Then breathe out as slowly as you can.
Repeat this five to seven times.

When 'relaxation' becomes a habit, it helps us to lead our lives 'easily'.

Regular relaxation creates a stress-free body and mind.

When we maintain a stress-free state, our limits are clear to us.

The moment we lose this state of mind, we start to ignore our own boundaries.

We then allow others to violate them.

MEMORY, NEGATIVE EMOTIONS AND STRESS

Memory is coloured by negative emotions.
Stress, created by negative emotions such as anger
and fear, impairs memory.
Getting rid of anger and fear frees our memory
and improves our concentration.

Memory and concentration are impaired in many mental conditions. This is mostly due to stress.

Anger and fear are classical stress-creating emotions.

It stands to reason that concentration and memory will improve when we release such negative emotions from our body systems.

Clinical experience shows this to be true.

RESTING THE BRAIN

*The easiest way to achieve relaxation is to shut off
all our senses simultaneously. It is simple to do,
once we acquire the skill.*

If we close our eyes and sit still with our minds
blank, our brain shuts down its activity temporarily.

This rests our brain.

This sense of relaxation is then conveyed to the rest
of the body.

Shutting off our senses is difficult for someone
unused to this principle.

But it can be achieved by practice.

SPEED

Speed burns us up – mentally and physically.
Slowness conserves mental and physical energy.
Regularly slowing down in life, after appropriate
intervals lived at a fast pace, is one secret of
success.

In Nature, haste is mandatory when our survival is threatened. The living body then has to produce a lot of energy to deal with the threat.

The more energy we use up, the more wear and tear the body undergoes.

Our bodies then become dysfunctional – either by death or by becoming unstable.

Intermittently slowing down – or even stopping completely – is helpful.

STRESS AND MATERIALISM

The more stressed-out we are, the more materialistic we become. The more relaxed we are, the more spiritual we become.
Balance between materialism and spirituality brings happiness.

Clinical experience shows that stress brings about a sense of insecurity.

This creates a desire to make ourselves more powerful than others.

Money and social status then become important.

This in turn makes us hoarders. We then like to hoard money and buy bigger houses and cars.

As stress (both emotional and physical) diminishes, we feel less need to hoard.

When we become relaxed, even the atheists and agnostics among us become spiritual.

STRESS AND VICTORY

A stressed-out individual likes to win by making others look small. A relaxed individual wins while allowing everyone to experience a sense of victory.

Stress is a sign of insecurity. Stressed-out people fear for their survival. So their tendency is to 'hit back' with aggression. Such people insult others and shout at them.

Unknown to themselves, they have a tendency to make others feel and look small – so that they themselves can look big.

Relaxed individuals are confident, secure and encouraging. They will allow others to grow and become big. In return they become bigger themselves.

A winner at heart can usually make others win.

TURNING STRESS INTO A CHALLENGE

The moment that we come to regard a stressful situation as a challenge, we experience a fall in our stress levels (including cortisol, the stress hormone).

Research shows that our attitude to any situation determines how we feel about it. Our attitude can make us relaxed about a situation that could be considered stressful.

When we look upon a stressful situation as a challenge, the mind ceases to think of it as stressful.

This results in a fall in our blood cortisol levels.

Cortisol is a hormone that increases in our blood when we are under stress.

TWO-MINUTE RELAXATION

Close your eyes.

Then imagine a wave of relaxation spreading downwards
from the top of your head.

Imagine it spreading slowly over your whole body, front
and back, top to bottom – down towards your toes.

Slowly visualise this sensation moving along your body,
until finally it reaches your toes.

Then open your eyes.

Tips
On
Spiritual
Health

BELIEF IN GOD

It is not necessary to believe in God in order to be spiritual. An atheist can be a spiritual person too.

A spiritual person is generous, trusting, forgiving, sharing and is able to give without expecting anything in return.

Although these qualities develop naturally with spiritual practices, they can also be present in someone who does not believe in God.

Trust in humanity and goodness of spirit are also seen in non-religious people.

DEATH

Death may seem to us to be an end. But for Nature it is the completion of a process that begins with our birth.

Most of us are afraid of death. Our fear may be a fear of pain, rather than a fear of death itself. This fear may be unfounded, because death may be painless.

From Nature's perspective, life is a process. It has a beginning, middle and an end.

For us it is the 'unknown' aspect – whence we came and where we are going – that makes us fearful of death. For Nature, death is just a process.

EVIL

Evil involves putting the self-interest of the few
above the interests of the rest of humankind.

Goodness is widespread. The reason for this is that Nature operates on the principle of "goodness for everyone."

Evil is not the norm. It manifests itself in isolation. Anything that is done "only" for the benefit of the few, to the detriment of others, is evil.

Negative emotions and greed, usually lie behind such actions.

The interests of humankind – and the universe – override the interests of the few. So truth or goodness always wins out over evil.

FORGIVENESS

*Only those who consider themselves to be mentally
stronger, more generous but not superior than others, can
truly forgive. A weak-minded person uses forgiveness to
survive.*

Some people believe they have forgiven another
person simply by speaking the words of forgiveness.

As long as we continue to hold anger and fear
within our bodies, it is almost impossible to carry a feeling
of forgiveness for someone who has hurt us.

Only by first getting rid of our own fears and anger,
can we get a sense of forgiveness.

When this happens, the offender appears small and
insignificant, in our mental picture of him, or her.

FREEDOM

Choices come with freedom.
When enslaved by emotions, our lives become
stereotyped, boring and stagnant.
It is our duty to free ourselves of such slavery.

People would generally like to have more choices, giving them more freedom to express themselves.

This can be achieved only if we have little emotional attachment to our past.

We are, in truth, emotional slaves.

As soon as we free ourselves of past emotions, we experience the freedom that comes with having more options.

As long as we remain stuck emotionally to our past, we are unable to fulfil our potential.

HEAVEN AND HELL

A place where all is in balance could be Heaven.
Hell could be a place of extremes.

Balance between opposing forces is essential to happiness.

A place where there is justice, enough wealth and a moderate climate, would be heavenly.

Too much of anything creates imbalance. Too much misery, too much heat, too much cold, too little money – all can make life hell.

Even too much of wealth can create hell.

LETTING GO

Letting go is a core feature of Nature.
She lets go of her abundance, to enable us to
receive.

When we let go control of children, emotions, sadness, grief or anger, at appropriate moments and in appropriate ways, we make way for happiness.

A lake from which no-one draws water stagnates.

As we too stagnate, if we hold on for too long to what has been given to us.

NATURE'S ETHICS

The standards that Nature sets down for us are higher than the highest standards advocated by our parents or any institution.

Life operates at two levels – physical and spiritual, seen and unseen.

The standards of conduct that we learn from fellow humans, are the ones normally imposed upon us.

Members of any profession, for example, are expected to conduct themselves according to certain standards laid down by other humans.

The standards set down by Nature, however, are higher than any man-made ethic.

In order to be aware of Nature's standards, we only need to apply ourselves regularly to meditation or relaxation.

Our standards of conduct are then raised instinctively.

NATURE HELPS
THE BIGGER CAUSE

In the struggle between benefits for the few and freedom for the many, Nature is always supportive of the bigger cause.

As time moves on, a pattern develops with most things in life.

In the present scientific age, most patterns are understood in scientific terms. This has given some people with special scientific knowledge, power over others. Such power is bound to be abused at times.

When such an abuse occurs, freedom-loving people oppose it.

In the struggle that follows, the cause that benefits most people 'wins'. Then the new order inevitably takes over.

RELIGION
AND SPIRITUALITY

Sometimes we get confused between religion and spirituality.
All religions are born out of spirituality – but not vice versa.

Spiritual Laws are Natural Laws. They have existed since the birth of the universe.

Each religion has picked up only some of these Laws. So, most religions are limited in scope.

There are many Laws – and there is much knowledge – extending beyond religion.

We can appreciate this only when we expand ourselves mentally, to experience the spirituality that transcends all religions.

Accepting ourselves generates a respect for ourselves. When that happens, we find it easier to show respect for others.

SPIRITUAL FREEDOM

The beautiful thing about spiritual freedom is that the freer we are, the more responsible we become towards society at large.

It is strange, yet true, that we need man-made laws to ensure that people respect the rights of others.

However, a truly spiritual person has no need to be so restrictive and controlling.

The freer a person feels in their spirit, the more positive they are towards society at large. They are more inclined to contribute, than to extract.

The material needs of such people are few.

SPIRITUAL PEOPLE

It is sign of a spiritual person to be modern in every age.
A hundred years from today such a person would accept the changes in society over the century.
They would still be happy in themselves.

Paradoxically, a spiritual person lives with the changing times, while spirituality itself is a very ancient concept.

A spiritual person remains mentally young for a longer period. To be able to adapt quickly in a changing world is a sign of such a person.

'Acceptance' is the characteristic quality of someone spiritual.

SPIRITUALITY AS SCIENCE

Science is the art of asking the right questions at the right time.
Science transforms experience into knowledge. But too much science can make us intellectually and spiritually blind and deaf.

Science enables us to seek answers to questions currently unanswered.

In order to learn through science, we need to experiment. Experimentation is experience.

The experience then becomes documented and accepted fact.

However, we can be straitjacketed by such factual knowledge and lose our freedom to experiment further.

This stunts our intellectual and spiritual growth.

In order to maintain a scientific approach we need constantly to be curious – and to keep experimenting. This is true of spirituality too.

TIME IS PRECIOUS

Our most vital asset in 'life' is time.

Lack of time is the biggest source of stress in the industrialised world.

When we speak of our 'life' we refer to the time during which we are alive. Time before or after our own existence, has no relevance for us.

Yet people who live life at a fast pace lack time to spend with their partners and families.

This lack of time is the major source of family breakdown.

UNCONDITIONAL LOVE

Love is a positive feeling. It is therefore the opposite of hate, anger, guilt and fear. It can be conditional or unconditional.

When we fall in love we are blinded by the other person's good qualities and we don't see their weaknesses.

When we become more familiar with this person, we sometimes start to fall out of love with them. In reality, this has more to do with our own issues than with the other person's weaknesses.

If we work through our own issues, we can fall in love again. This time, unconditionally.

Conditional love seeks security. But if our love is unconditional, we can give a sense of security to others.

Conditional love is possessive. Unconditional love gives freedom.

WHEN PRAYERS
ARE ANSWERED

Prayer is answered in two situations:
1. When our five senses are calm simultaneously.
2. When all our senses are stimulated to the
maximum simultaneously, as when our lives are
under threat.

Some people pray as a formality. Others pray to convey thanks, or to ask for what they desire. The way we pray affects the response we receive.

When we are without any negative emotions – like anger, fear, hatred or jealousy – our senses are calm.

When we feel threatened, our senses are sharpened.

Both these states are hypnotic. It is under these conditions that we get the best results. It would be worth our while to experiment with this.

What
To
Do
About
Your
Emotional
Health

ANGER
IMPAIRS THOUGHT

Anger diminishes the blood flow to our brains.

Research shows that when we get angry, our blood vessels become narrower.

This decreases the flow of blood to the brain, thus reducing the supply to the brain of food and oxygen.

This limits our thinking processes and we then lose our ability to think clearly.

AVOIDANCE OF TRUTH

Avoidance of our feelings is like avoiding truth.
Truth is so powerful that it withstands all odds.
However hard we suppress our feelings, the truth
expresses itself in our actions and words.

Although science has made progress in many areas, it has overlooked the significance of feelings and emotions. Most of the killing in this world is due to anger that someone has held on to, for far too long.

The way we feel is expressed in the way we walk, talk, think and behave. Truth reveals itself in one form or another.

DEALING WITH ANGER

Anger causes stress in the body.
Dealing with anger regularly, helps to clear our
bodies of the accumulation of toxic chemicals,
produced by our metabolisms through stress.
The body's physiology then becomes more flexible.

When you feel anger for someone, do the following exercise:

1. Close your eyes and imagine seeing the person you are angry with.

2. In your imagination, treat that person – in word and deed – as you would like to treat them in real life.

3. Repeat the words and deeds in your imagination as many times as necessary, until you calm down.

BURNING ANGER

The scriptures tell us that anger kills us.
Science tells us that we secrete more of the stress
hormone cortisol when we are angry.
Cortisol is now known as 'the death hormone.'

Anger is said to 'burn' our body.

It is a negative emotion that prepares us to fight a stressful situation successfully.

The scriptures warn us that anger is destructive. Scientific research now confirms this.

EMOTIONAL ENERGY

Emotional energy is like heat. It needs to burn itself out, before it starts to burn us and those around us.

Any negative or unpleasant emotion creates stress in our physiological processes. Physiologically, the body responds to a negative emotion by gearing up to face a danger that may or may not exist. This process must end before the body can create more energy.

However, we are not being taught the skills we need to complete the process.

This leads to an accumulation of negative emotional energy in our body systems. It begins to affect our behaviour and our outlook on life in general.

EMOTIONAL HEALING

Emotional healing is a spontaneous, natural process. We can accelerate it through skilful guidance.

Healing of any kind is a natural process.

No matter how ground-breaking a medical achievement may be, the healing process is still controlled by Nature. At best, we can only help this process by preventing infection, or by joining together broken tissues.

Similarly, emotional healing is a natural process. It takes time to complete it. However, it can be speeded-up through guidance; or slowed-down by suppressing our negative emotions.

EMOTION RULES

Emotions rule our thinking, as well as our behaviour and how we see the world around us. Any decision we make in our personal lives, depends on how we feel at that moment in time.

It is wrongly believed that emotions can always be controlled or changed by thinking.

If violent and angry people could 'think' away their anger, there would be hardly any violence.

Paranoid people 'think' they are threatened by others, because of their own fears.

It is our *feelings* that determine how we *think*, at any moment in time.

FEELING OUR WAY
TO HAPPINESS

If thinking could only solve our emotional difficulties, everyone could think themselves to happiness.

We have been taught to believe that the ability to think is what differentiates us from other animals.

However, attempting to change the way we feel through thinking is a fruitless exercise.

Even if successful, this approach would be temporary and would use up too much time and energy.

It is impossible to *think* ourselves to happiness.

Happiness can be *felt*. It is an experience.

GRIEF OF LETTING GO

*We take for granted something we have had for a
long time.
When it is time to let it go we resist the change and
grieve over it.
This is also true of anger, fear and stress.*

When we have held on to something for a long
time, we get used to it. This is equally true of our
relationships and our emotions.

We grieve for the loss of our near and dear ones.

But getting rid of anger, fear, guilt, hatred and
jealousy, has the same kind of impact on us.

When we let these emotions go, our bodies behave
as if they are grieving over their loss.

Letting go such feelings is a painful process. It takes
time to complete it.

PRAYER

When you ask the Lord for something, imagine how you would respond if your own child asked you for the same thing, using the same language.

Prayer is either a request, or an acknowledgement of what we already have.

If a child needs something, it asks a parent for it.

Throwing tantrums is unhelpful.

Threats are unhelpful too.

In prayer, while making a request, some people get angry with the Lord.

Obviously, in this case, the chances of the request being granted are slim.

HAPPINESS

Happiness is a state of mind. It can be achieved with little money and minimum needs.

Someone with few material possessions and fewer physical needs can be a happy person.

As our needs diminish, our expectations in life can easily be met. This brings about a sense of contentment, which is sometimes called happiness.

Happiness is unrelated to our wealth, our earning power or our social status. It is a state of mind.

HAPPINESS AND GROWTH

Anything that brings happiness, prosperity and growth to everyone is bound to grow itself. That is the law of Nature.

We inherently know that "goodness" wins and that "evil" is eventually destroyed.

"Goodness" enables others to feel free and to grow.

Any activity that brings about growth in others is bound to bring happiness too.

Such activities are widely supported by Nature.

Anything that opposes such growth and happiness is eventually destroyed.

HAPPINESS SPREADS

Happiness, like stress, is contagious.
A happy person will spread happiness in their
family or organisation.

A happy person is more confident, more productive, more grounded and more generous than an unhappy person.

Only a happy person can successfully be responsible for spreading happiness.

A happy person is therefore the best representative of any family, corporation or country.

HOLDING ON
TO ANGER

Holding on to anger generates fear, then guilt.
This can lead to panic and phobias.
Phobias can lead to paranoia and a loss of touch
with reality.

It is important that we develop skills to dissipate our anger as soon as it is generated.

This needs to be done constructively without harming ourselves or others.

INFLUENCE OF EMOTION

No matter how logical, reasonable or literate we are, our decision-making is still governed by our emotional make-up.

We live in an age where much emphasis is placed on literacy and education.

However, despite all our training and skills, our decision-making remains governed by our emotions.

We perceive our environment through a screen of emotion.

The lighter the emotional baggage that we carry, the less likely we are to regard any situation to be stressful.

Our emotions can make us prejudicial and judgmental.

LEARNING FROM EMOTIONAL EXPERIENCES

When we let go the feelings associated with any emotional experience, that experience is transformed into a lesson.

As long as an experience is remembered with attached emotions, it remains vivid in our memories.

If emotions are burnt out, expressed or released, the remembered experience loses its intensity.

It is then remembered as a 'realisation', or lesson.

PAST, PRESENT, FUTURE

Our Present is happy with an emotionally cleaned-up Past.
An emotionally cleaned-up Present facilitates a happy Future.

Happiness has little to do with our environment or circumstances.

Emotions are crucial to happiness or unhappiness.

We all have the ability to burn out the energy of our negative emotions.

When we do this for our Past, the Past becomes insignificant. It ceases to be carried over into our Present.

When we have little or no emotional baggage from our Past, our energies become focused on the Now.

We become happy and adaptable to our Present.

When that happens, our Future becomes hopeful and positive.

POWER OF EMOTION

Our emotions always influence our thinking –
sometimes destructively.

Some of us believe, probably erroneously, that we think only with our brains.

The way our brains function reflects our emotional make-up.

Many psychopaths, for instance, think destructively because of the emotional effects of trauma in their lives.

Generous, philanthropic people, think of helping others because they feel the emotion of love for humanity.

The power of emotions is greater than the power of the intellect.

Intellect is wasted when used to suppress negative emotions.

Intellect without negative emotions is "wisdom."

RECIPE FOR HAPPINESS

The recipe for happiness is simple.
Minimum needs. Enough work to meet those needs.
Close friends. Close family members. Good health.
Enough time to enjoy all these.

Happiness is a state of mind that transcends worldly possessions.

Even a person with few worldly possessions can attain happiness.

The fewer the needs of any person, the happier that person becomes.

The advantage of having fewer needs is that "little" is often "enough."

SADNESS

Sadness is an emotional stage that precedes acceptance.

In the process of accepting change in our lives, we may go through stages of denial, anger and sadness.

In order to accept change, either in our external environment or within ourselves, we must first experience sadness.

We feel sad when we let go of anger and fear.

After sadness lifts, the new situation becomes more acceptable to us.

PRINCIPLE OF GROWTH

Whatever promotes the economic, personal and spiritual development of an individual, a society or humankind, is bound to succeed – despite obstacles.

The universe operates on the simple principle of reciprocal growth.

If you take up a short or a long-term project that promotes the growth of others – and of yourself – universal forces will help you to complete it.

Those forces will also destroy anything that is done with only self-interest in mind.

Why not go ahead and experiment with this principle?

PROBLEM SOLVING

Problems are best solved by taking these steps:

1. Stop struggling with the problem.
2. Acknowledge the existence of the problem.
3. Ask yourself: 'What is the pattern to the problem?' Then spend time looking at the pattern before you master it.
4. Look at ways to change that pattern.

Destruction and conflict are always the last resorts in solving any problem.

SLAVES TO NEGATIVITY

*Unknown to us, we are all slaves to the negativity
in our pasts.
Freedom from this slavery brings about growth for
everyone around us.*

When we work through our anger and grief, we experience a sense of physical freedom. Some of us may then just shrug our shoulders and say we 'feel different.'

Negative emotions seem to grip us, mind and body.

This grip is loosened when unfinished emotional work has been completed.

The sense of freedom this brings creates a new but positive way of thinking.

Our perceptions change. Then, spontaneously, we are able to let people around us grow.

How
To
Improve
Your
Relationship
With
The World

BELIEFS, ACTIONS AND RESPONSIBILITY

We have every right to our beliefs and to act upon them.
Such actions are followed by consequences.
We are responsible for these consequences, however unpleasant they may be for us.

Our belief systems can make us rigid in our thinking. This results in our behaviour becoming stereotyped.

Each of us has a right to believe what we want to believe.

But when we take actions based on such beliefs – actions that affect our own lives and the lives of others – we are responsible for the results.

CREATIVITY

Creativity is all about freedom.
How many people have you seen at their creative
peak, working within a rigid system?
Systems are sets of rules that can stifle creativity.

Creativity is an expression of freedom.

Creativity can flourish only if the creator feels free. This feeling of freedom can also be nourished by the environment someone works in. If a creative person is bound by too many rules, their creativity diminishes.

POWER AND SERVICE

Many of the scriptures say that power is given to us to serve others.
They also say that those who serve are given power.
Power and service grow in proportion to each other.

Power, or strength, comes to anyone who has a will to serve others – selflessly.

Mother Teresa started her mission single-handed. Her power to help others increased as her willingness to serve them grew.

With increased service comes an increase in power.

In Nature the only use for power is service.

Power for the sake of dominating others is counterproductive.

RIGHTS AND RESPONSIBILITIES

Our rights can be wrongs, if we ignore our responsibilities in any situation.

We all have rights based on the laws of the land we live in.

Our rights are balanced by our responsibilities to the State. We are supposed to be aware of them. Ignorance of their existence is an unacceptable excuse for not following them.

Similarly, acquiring knowledge of Nature's laws is our responsibility. However, we often make excuses for our behaviour in the belief that these laws do not exist.

We pay the price for such ignorance with unhappiness and suffering.

SCIENTIFIC LEARNING

Some believe scientific learning must be tightly controlled along accepted lines.
But it is also scientific to learn through new observations – even if unconventional.

Whenever anything new is discovered, learnt or observed, the scientists among us test it along 'scientific' lines, to see if it conforms to collectively accepted 'fact' and convention.

It is often only the more open-minded who dare to give credence to the new finding.

Most may follow the 'herd mentality' and accept the new finding *only* if and when it is tested to their satisfaction, against traditional scientific wisdom.

Respect and recognition come only to those who dare to look at things differently.

PEACE

History shows that nations prosper during prolonged periods of peace. The same is true for individuals. They also prosper when at peace with themselves.

In the universe, microcosm mirrors macrocosm.

Nations prosper during prolonged periods of peace.

A nation in turmoil gets destroyed. Persistent conflict results in poverty.

Individual lives follow the same principle.

Peace of mind stimulates creativity and action that lead to growth. The individual then prospers and can help others to prosper too.

HOLD AND LOSE
LET GO AND HAVE

*Isn't it strange that the more we try to hold on to
things and relationships, the more we lose them?
The more we let go, the more we have.
This is also true of the control we seek in our lives.*

Clinical experience shows that our insecurities make us hold on to money, emotions, relationships and jobs.

Once we feel secure, we *willingly* let them go.

A sense of security brings a freedom that enables us to see more options.

The less we desire control, the more secure we are.

It is ironic that the less we pursue control, the more of it we will have.

Some
Points
Of
Worldly Wisdom

CHANGE

*People who refuse to change are simply exercising
their right to suffer.*

Life changes from moment to moment. We have to
learn to change with these moments.

This is called adaptability. Those who fail to adapt
create suffering for themselves and for others. In order to
minimise our mental suffering, we have to change with the
times – and to accept that change.

CONFUSION

Confusion belongs to a state of transition.
Take important decisions only when you have
come through this state, otherwise you may regret
them.

Confusion occurs when we drift from one mind-set to another. It is a state of transition.

We are confused when we start to think differently than before.

Although we may lack clear thinking during our confused state, we may subsequently move forward towards clear thinking. The decisions we take in this clear state are then quite different to what they would have been before.

EASY LIFE

If you can accomplish something easily, why work hard for it?

Our life becomes as easy as we make it.

Hard work involves effort. It is mandatory to work hard to survive. When our survival is threatened, we spontaneously and naturally work hard, using a lot of energy.

As we become easy with life, we use less energy to achieve the same result as before.

From Nature's perspective, it is the regularity of work that achieves goals, rather than the force that is used.

CRYING
STRENGTHENS US

As we cry outside, we become stronger inside.
People who put on a brave face, may tend to live
with pain and hurt in their hearts.

Crying is an excellent exercise to strengthen our nervous systems. It helps us to cleanse our negative emotions. This results in better acceptance of emotional issues when the crying is over.

People who suppress their painful emotions hold on to their tears. Only when they allow themselves to cry do they release their emotions.

Stressed-out people have difficulty in crying.

Relaxed individuals do it easily, if not readily.

CULTURE AND LEADERSHIP

*The culture of a family, corporation or institution,
is mirrored in the way those at its head think and
act.*

There is an old saying in India: 'As is the King, so are the subjects'. It goes without saying that a member of a family or an organisation will learn the standards set by people at the top.

It is unlikely that corruption will survive for long in any culture if those at the top are honest.

If you want to study the standards of any organisation you may save time and energy by looking first at its leader. Learn of the person and you will learn of the organisation.

EVERYTHING ENDS

It is a universal truth that everything that has a
beginning also has an ending.
Thus our negative feelings – no matter how painful
– will also come to an end.

Everything that is born, dies. Anything that has a beginning also has an ending. Anything with a starting point has an end point.

Our feelings and emotions have their lives too. We tend to hide negative emotions to avoid feeling them. In this way they continue to live.

But if we have the courage to face these emotions – if we feel them and challenge them – they die. It is inevitable.

EXPANSION

Expansion has a unique quality.
If you encourage people to expand intellectually
and professionally under your supervision you will
find yourself spontaneously enriched.

Imagine yourself to be like a large inflated balloon inside of which are smaller inflated balloons.

If somehow these smaller balloons are expanded further, the larger balloon expands spontaneously.

When you allow people to grow professionally, individually and intellectually, their status and self-respect increases.

Only confident and secure people can permit such development in others.

EXPERIENCING LIFE

Whatever other people or books may tell us about life we really only learn about it through our own experience.

Our experience is our greatest teacher. Show a toddler a burning candle and tell him or her that the flame burns. The child will still attempt to catch the flame.

Take the child's hand to let it experience briefly the burning heat of the flame. The child will quickly withdraw the hand, having learnt its lesson.

We all are like children. We learn only from experience.

This is one reason why wise people encourage us to discover the Natural laws for ourselves. People who are ignorant of these laws criticise them, without having the courage to experience them.

EXPERIENCING SPIRITUALITY

All religions are spiritual, but spirituality itself is beyond any religion.

Spirituality concerns the core truth on which the universe is based.

This truth involves laws that govern the systems of the universe, beyond the comprehension of our intellects.

We may experience some awareness of these laws in the practise of meditation.

If such awareness could be given to us in book form, then each one of us would become an Enlightened One.

Spirituality is an experience – a feeling – that defies description. If you dare to experience it, you will simply flow with it. But if you try to become its owner, you will be destined to fail.

FAITH

Faith is the beautiful combination of trust and will.
It can move mountains by making them molehills.

      Faith has a sense of trust about it. If we have faith in someone, we *trust* that person.

      Belief involves a conscious decision.

      Faith is an unconscious and positive feeling. It has power to create miracles in our lives.

      The *belief* in our ability to achieve something is the first step towards having *faith* in ourselves.

GENERATING
MISERY AND LOVE

*People who create misery, anger and fear in
others, are themselves experiencing such pain.
Those who are confident and who have love for
themselves, generate the same feelings in others.*

It is virtually impossible to make others miserable
and fearful, without having these emotions oneself.

Such people, because of their own insecurity,
display domineering behaviour towards others.

Those who respect themselves, also respect others.

Getting there is a painful task. Only those who dare
to reach those depths will win.

HEAD AND HEART

If the head ruled the heart, we would all be robots.

We live in a world that particularly values intellectual intelligence.

Despite this, many creative people, by using their imaginations, have helped to change the world.

Logic, when used too much, prevents a person from experiencing life's ups and downs.

We need a balance between our intellect and our emotions otherwise we will be just like machines.

KNOWLEDGE OR WISDOM?

Knowledge and wisdom are different.
Knowledge can be obtained by reading.
Applying that knowledge brings experience.

But using this experience to solve problems in an
exceptional way is a mark of wisdom.

People who read a lot sometimes gather the impression that they are wiser than others.

Knowledge of a subject does not always mean that we have the ability needed to apply that knowledge in the field.

Knowledge may come from books. Wisdom comes from life's experiences.

A wise person can use knowledge in a more creative and useful way than others.

LIFE IS A STAGE

If all the world's a stage,
Most of us are players
Who don't know their own lines.

These words may parody Shakespeare but they also make a lot of sense.

Clinical experience shows that most of us carry on with our lives with no sense of direction.

This is because we act out the lines written for us by our parents. These lines are ingrained in our body systems in the form of emotions and feelings – both positive and negative.

When we drop the negative emotions scripted by our parents our lives change direction.

MAKING MISTAKES

*Nature allows us to make mistakes – and in the
process she lets us learn from life.
It falls to us to give ourselves permission to make
our mistakes.*

The only way to learn in life is by making mistakes.
They may be made by others or by ourselves.

Some of us go through the painful process of
seeking perfection to prevent ourselves from making
mistakes.

Fortunately we are all imperfect in some ways.
Those of us who are happy with this fact learn from
mistakes quickly.

Those who are afraid of making mistakes have
difficulty learning from life's experiences.

POVERTY
ENCOURAGES SHARING

Poverty may be a curse.
But it is a blessing when it keeps families together
and encourages people to share.

Shortage of money can create physical discomfort.
Sometimes it can also deprive us of basic amenities.
People then tend to share what they have with each other.

This creates a bond which keeps people together.

Lots of money provides individual freedom, but it also isolates individuals from their near and dear ones.

The need to share with others diminishes as a result.

ROLE OF THE PAST

Our Present is determined by the effect our Past has upon us. Our Future is determined by our Present.
Is it then a coincidence that people who are depressed about their Past can also be anxious about their Future?

Some of the people are 'taught' to live in the Now – the Present. So they come to believe that their Past no longer plays a significant role in their Present.
How wrong they are.

The Past haunts them like a frightful ghost. But if they neutralise its negative influence, the Past will become positive.

Its influence on their Present is then positive. It enables them to live in the Now – without bothering about the Past, or worrying about the Future.

If they are preoccupied with fears from the Past, their Present will begin to trouble their Future.

MONEY

Money is a means to a comfortable life.
In excess it brings discomfort to ourselves and to
others.
Only wisdom keeps us within the bounds of
moderation.

Man created money to facilitate the exchange of skills, services and commodities. Its importance still lies only in facilitating such exchange.

When money becomes a goal in its own right it creates stress in individuals and in any system to which they belong.

If our needs are few they are easily achieved. If money comes to us beyond what we require to fulfil such needs, then it can easily be shared with others.

MORE FREEDOM
MORE CHOICE

Our whole struggle in life is to attain freedom of spirit to increase the options open to us.

We spend our lives seeking an elusive happiness.

We feel happy when our spirit feels free of sadness, of illness, of anger, of hurt, of pain.

When we feel free we develop an ability to create and see new choices.

Without this sense of freedom our choices become limited.

OLD AGE

Where there is disrespect for old age, spiritual degeneration sets in.

Macrocosm and microcosm are related.

But microcosm is subservient to macrocosm.

Lower life forms are subservient to higher ones.

Higher life forms are not only bigger they also have longer life spans.

God is presumed to be the biggest being of all, with the longest life span – omnipresent, omniscient and eternal.

Nature operates on a hierarchical basis with bigger and older creatures deserving the respect of smaller and younger ones.

Showing disrespect to old age goes against the flow of Nature.

Where this happens, spiritual degeneration is bound to set in.

POSITIVE THINKING

*Positive thinking results spontaneously from the
release of negative emotions.*

Our thinking has its roots in our emotions.

The way we *feel* about a subject determines what
we *think* of it.

With guilt, for instance, we think badly of
ourselves.

Once the guilt is removed we respect ourselves.
Then we start to think positively.

This can be achieved without affirmations or
assertiveness training.

Positive thinking can be developed *spontaneously*
without *forcing* ourselves to think positively.

WISDOM

Wisdom is an innate quality that we all share.
When we have the courage to tap into our own
wisdom we bring its rewards to ourselves and to
others.

Clinical experience shows that wisdom is inherent in us all. It lies buried under the layers of emotional injuries that we experience in life.

We can all tap into this universal wisdom or awareness, but only if we let go of our negative emotions.

When we exploit our wisdom, our lives and the lives of those around us, become richer in many ways.

VIOLENCE

Violent behaviour is the motor activity of our feelings of anger.
If the anger is burnt out violence subsides.

Violent behaviour is the product of an angry heart.

Where there is no anger there is no violence.

Any human violence we see in everyday life is the result of suppressed anger.

If the anger is burnt out, violent behaviour simply stops.

The suppression of anger does not help to diminish violent behaviour.

TYRANNY
OF THE NORM

The term 'Abnormal' is applied pejoratively at times to something of a higher standard than the 'Norm.'

'Norm' is a word often used to describe the 'generality,' or 'normality.'

Anything outside the common stream in life is an 'exception.' An 'exception' is not of course the 'norm'. It is outside the 'general' run of life.

In many situations anything better than the 'general' or 'norm' – in any sphere of life – is also considered to be 'abnormal' in a pejorative sense.

Children of above average intelligence are sometimes labelled in this way.

It is not always appreciated that what is 'abnormal' can be a very positive exception.

The norms of society are not necessarily Nature's norms.

The 'abnormal' of society could be Nature's gift.

THINKING CHANGES
AS FEELINGS CHANGE

It is extraordinary that a change in our emotional make-up entirely alters how we see ourselves and others.
It also alters our way of thinking and our ability to make decisions.

Emotions influence our thinking and the way in which we perceive the world around us.

If we are emotionally neutral we can think in an impartial manner. Our perception is then non-judgemental.

It is noteworthy that neither logic nor distraction can change how we feel for long.

Conversely, however, if our emotional make-up changes, our thinking will change with it.

Our thinking depends on how we feel. As our feelings change, our thinking changes too.

STOP AND SUCCEED

In order to succeed in anything without getting stressed-out, we need to learn when to stop – and for how long.

When we set a goal we usually 'strive' to achieve it.

This requires effort. We need to spend energy in the process.

If we do not take adequate rest 'burn out' may occur.

In order to achieve a goal without stress, we need to take our time and to rest regularly from our activity.

Easy does it. Slow but steady always wins the race.

STANDARDS

It is amazing how frequently we lower standards in our personal and family lives in order to maintain high standards at work.

Struggling too hard to maintain high standards at work may be a sign of insecurity.

Standards can also be kept high without having to struggle.

If someone is so insecure as to be extremely focussed on work standards, there is bound to be some form of neglect in personal and family life.

This neglect results in difficulties all round.

Index

160

Recommended Reading

The Stress Barrier-Nature's Way To Overcoming Stress by Dr. Pradeep K Chadha published by Blackhall Publishing, Dublin. Ireland.

Hard To Stomach by Dr. John McKenna published by Newleaf Gill and McMillan Publishers, Dublin.Ireland.

The Essential Guide To Vaccinating Your Child by Dr. John McKenna published by Nutrition Research Centre.

Natural Alternatives to Antibiotics by Dr. John McKenna published by Newleaf Gill and McMillan Publishers, Dublin. Ireland.

Natural Alternatives To Tranquilizers by Dr. John McKenna published by Newleaf Gill and McMillan Publishers, Dublin. Ireland.

Beyond Prozac by Dr. Terry Lynch published by Marino Books , Dublin, Ireland.

Liberation By Oppression by Thomas Szas published by Transaction Publishers, USA.

Going Mad by Michael Corry published by Newleaf Gill and McMillan Publishers, Dublin, Ireland.

Depression An Emotion not a Disease by Dr.Michael Corry and Aine Tubridy published by Mercier Press, Dublin, Ireland.

Healing Without Freud or Prozac by David Serven-Schreiber published by Rodale International Ltd. USA.

Esteem for the Self: A Manual for Personal Transformation by Dr. N. Arrizza available for download at: http://www.telecoaching4u.com.

Printed in the United Kingdom
by Lightning Source UK Ltd.
125233UK00001B/76-171/A